AF599460

COOL CARS

LAMBORGHINI

COUNTACH

BY KAITLYN DULING

EPIC

BELLWETHER MEDIA ››› MINNEAPOLIS, MN

EPIC BOOKS are no ordinary books. They burst with intense action, high-speed heroics, and shadows of the unknown. Are you ready for an Epic adventure?

This edition first published in 2025 by Bellwether Media, Inc.

Library of Congress Cataloging-in-Publication Data

LC record for Lamborghini Countach available at:https://lccn.loc.gov/2024039204

Editor: Rachael Barnes Designer: Gabriel Hilger

Printed in the United States of America, North Mankato, MN.

TABLE OF CONTENTS

STANDOUT SPORTS CAR

Dozens of sports cars line up at the car show. Suddenly, a **rare** Lambo speeds down the street.

The Lamborghini Countach takes its place in line. Fans crowd around to get a closer look!

HOW DO YOU SAY THAT?

Said out loud, this Lambo model's name sounds like "koon-tash." In Italian, the word *countach* can mean "my goodness" or "wow!"

ALL ABOUT THE COUNTACH

LAMBORGHINI FACTORY IN ITALY

Lamborghini makes fast sports cars. The company started in Italy in 1963.

Lamborghinis, or Lambos, are also known for their standout looks. The Aventador and Miura are well-known **models**.

FAN FAVORITE

The Countachs of the 1970s were very popular. Today, some old Countach models sell for more than $1 million!

1976 COUNTACH

The first Countach was sold from 1974 to 1990.

It was built to look like it came from outer space! Fans loved its sharp angles and bright colors.

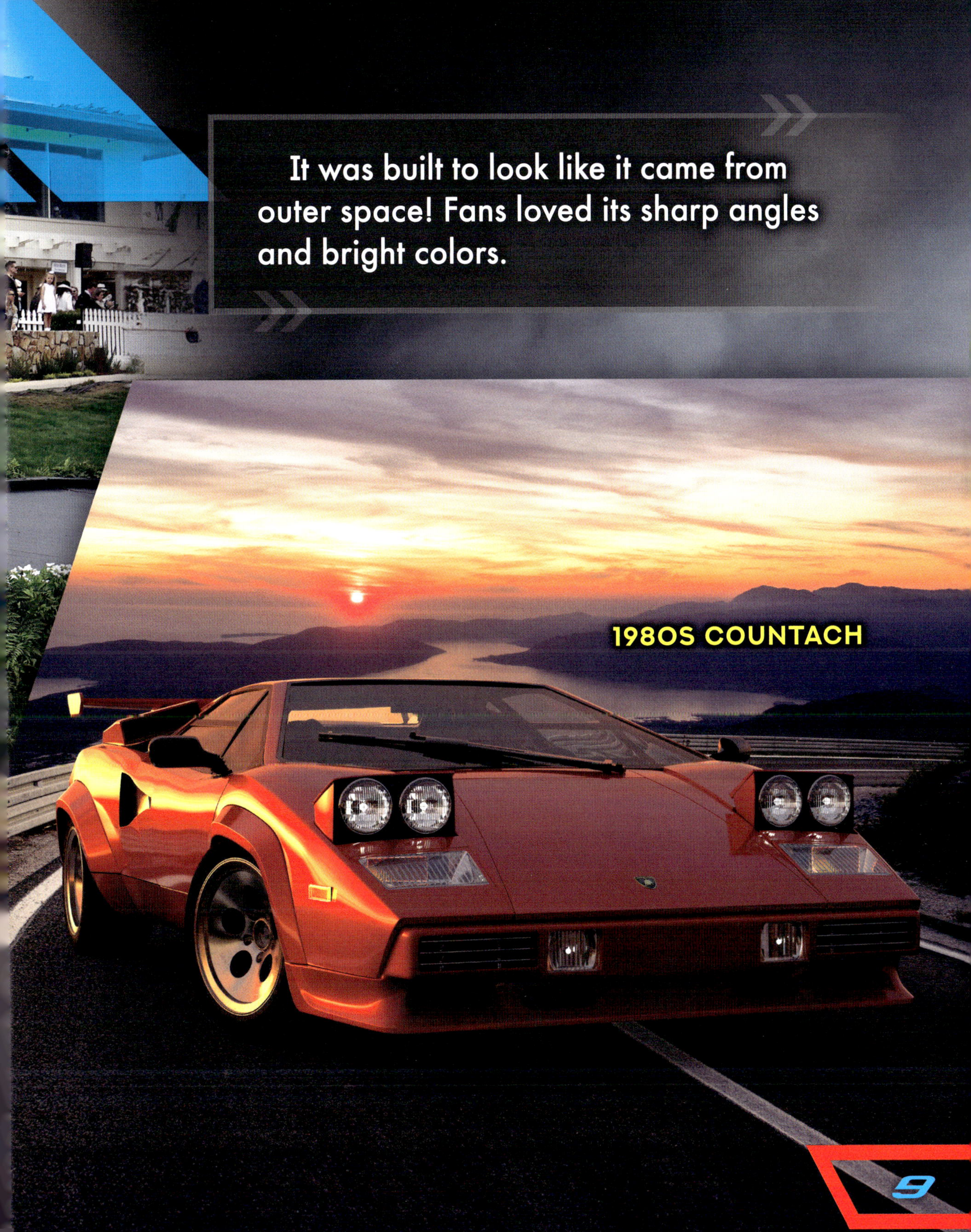

This car kept some of the original model's looks. But it is faster and more powerful.

2022 COUNTACH LPI 800-4

COUNTACH BASICS

YEAR FIRST MADE	1974
COST	started at $2.64 million in 2022
HOW MANY MADE	112 made in 2022

FEATURES

scissor doors

hexagonal wheel arches

side air intakes

PARTS OF THE COUNTACH

The Countach is a **hybrid** car. Its **V12 engine** pairs with an **electric motor**. Together they create 802 **horsepower**!

Each time the brakes are used, energy is stored. This helps power the motor.

ENGINE SPECS

V12 ENGINE AND AN ELECTRIC MOTOR

TOP SPEED	221 miles (355 kilometers) per hour
0-62 TIME	2.8 seconds
HORSEPOWER	802 hp

countach

The Countach has a wide shape, **rear diffuser**, and side **air intakes**. These **aerodynamic** features help the car drive faster.

SIZE CHART

Its lightweight body is made with **carbon fiber**. This gives it even more speed!

CARBON FIBER

SIDE AIR INTAKE

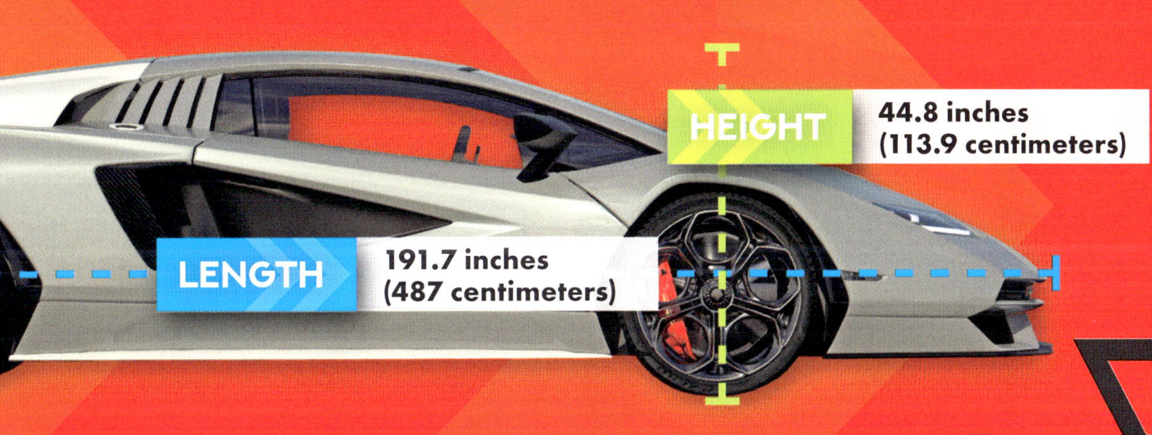

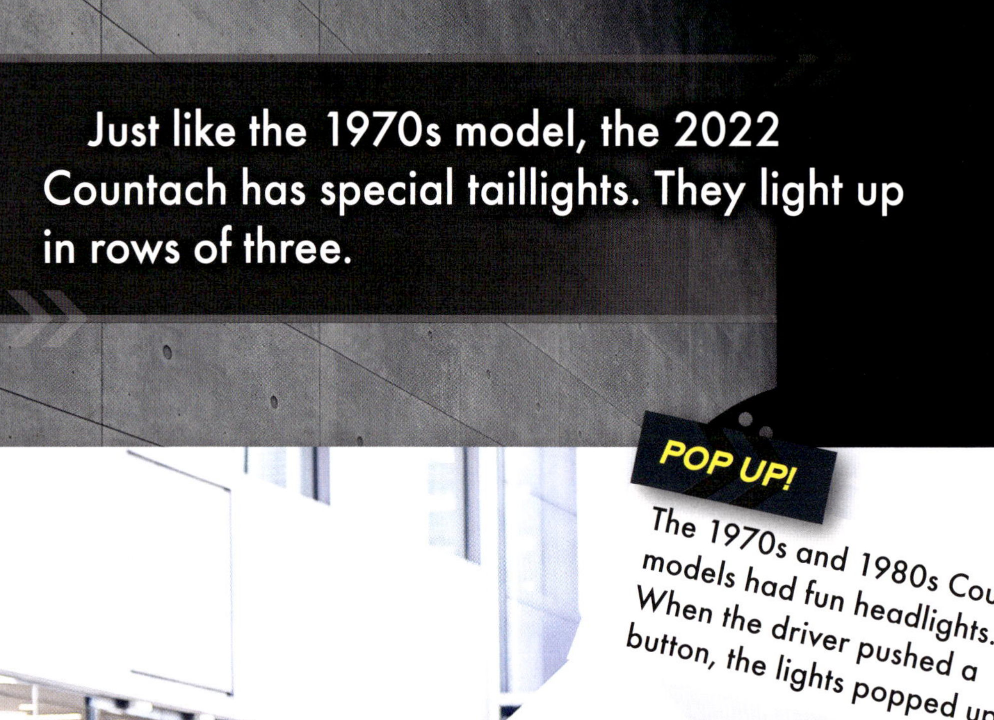

Just like the 1970s model, the 2022 Countach has special taillights. They light up in rows of three.

POP UP!

The 1970s and 1980s Countach models had fun headlights. When the driver pushed a button, the lights popped up!

TAILLIGHTS

The Countach has hidden handles that open its **scissor doors**. It also has **hexagonal** wheel arches.

Buyers had many choices to match the Countach to their style, including body color. There were more than 30 colors to choose from!

Inside, a button starts the car. Another button makes the sunroof appear clear or frosted.

THE COUNTACH'S FUTURE

Lamborghini sold all of the 2022 Countachs. But the Countach **inspired** parts of Lamborghini's first electric sports car.

The company is also working on a car that stores energy in its body! Lamborghini is speeding into the future.

LAMBORGHINI LANZADOR ELECTRIC SPORTS CAR

FUTURE ELECTRIC LAMBORGHINI

GLOSSARY

aerodynamic—able to move through air easily

air intakes—openings on a car that allow air to reach its engine

carbon fiber—a strong, lightweight material used to strengthen things

electric motor—a machine that gives something the power to move by using electricity

hexagonal—having six angles and six sides

horsepower—a measurement of the power of an engine or motor

hybrid—a car that uses both a gasoline engine and an electric motor for power

inspired—gave an idea about what to do or create

models—specific kinds of cars

rare—not found in large numbers

rear diffuser—a part on the back underside of a car that directs air and makes the car more aerodynamic

scissor doors—doors that open upwards, rather than outwards

V12 engine—an engine with 12 cylinders arranged in the shape of a "V"

TO LEARN MORE

AT THE LIBRARY

Adamson, Thomas K. *Lamborghini Huracán Evo.* Minneapolis, Minn.: Bellwether Media, 2023.

Colby, Jennifer. *Lamborghini.* Ann Arbor, Mich.: Cherry Lake Publishing, 2023.

Duling, Kaitlyn. *Lamborghini Aventador.* Minneapolis, Minn.: Bellwether Media, 2024.

ON THE WEB

FACTSURFER

Factsurfer.com gives you a safe, fun way to find more information.

1. Go to www.factsurfer.com.
2. Enter "Lamborghini Countach" into the search box and click 🔍.
3. Select your book cover to see a list of related content.

INDEX

The images in this book are reproduced through the courtesy of: ben bryant, front cover; Christian Santi/ Alamy, p. 3; Andia/ Contributor/ Getty Images, pp. 4, 14 (rear diffuser); Bloomberg/ Contributor/ Getty Images, pp. 5, 19, 20; CuorerouC, p. 6; Brandon Woyshnis, p. 7; Paul Pollock, p. 8; Mariusz Burcz/ Alamy, pp. 9, 11 (scissor doors, hexagonal wheel arches, side air intakes), 12, 15 (side air intake, length), 17 (hexagonal wheel arch), 21; Martyn Lucy/ Contributor/ Getty Images, pp. 10, 14 (width), 16; Dawid Swierczek/ Alamy, p. 11 (Lamborghini Countach); Bennnn/ Dreamstime.com, p. 13; Media Drum World via ZUMA Press, pp. 17 (scissor doors), 18.